In My Backyard

I SEE A SQUIRREL

By Alex Appleby

Gareth Stevens
Publishing

Please visit our website, www.garethstevens.com. For a free color catalog of all our high-quality books, call toll free 1-800-542-2595 or fax 1-877-542-2596.

Library of Congress Cataloging-in-Publication Data

Appleby, Alex.
  I see a squirrel / Alex Appleby.
    p. cm. – (In my backyard)
  Includes index.
  ISBN 978-1-4339-8560-7 (pbk.)
  ISBN 978-1-4339-8561-4 (6-pack)
  ISBN 978-1-4339-8559-1 (library binding)
  1. Squirrels—Juvenile literature. I. Title.
  QL737.R68N34 2013
  599.36—dc23
                                        2012022024

First Edition

Published in 2013 by
Gareth Stevens Publishing
111 East 14th Street, Suite 349
New York, NY 10003

Editor: Ryan Nagelhout
Designer: Katelyn Londino

Photo credits: Cover, pp. 1, 11 iStockphoto/Thinkstock.com; p. 5 Bill Mack/Shutterstock.com; p. 7 aspen rock/ Shutterstock.com; p. 9 Hemera/Thinkstock.com; pp. 13, 24 (teeth) John Czenke/Shutterstock.com; p. 15 James M Phelps, Jr/Shutterstock.com; p. 17 HGalina/Shutterstock.com; pp. 19, 24 (dens) ©iStockphoto.com/ lilly3; p. 21 USBFCO/Shutterstock.com; p. 23 Nicholas Jr/Photo Researchers/Getty Images; p. 24 (seeds) Comstock/Thinkstock.com.

Printed in the United States of America

CPSIA compliance information: Batch #CW13GS: For further information contact Gareth Stevens, New York, New York at 1-800-542-2595.

Contents

A squirrel is
a small rodent.

It has a long, furry tail.
It is very soft.

7

It moves very fast.

It runs away
from any danger.

It has four big front
teeth. They never
stop growing!

13

Big teeth help
squirrels eat.

15

It eats nuts, plants, and seeds.

A ground squirrel digs holes to live in.
These are called dens.

A tree squirrel hops
from tree to tree.
It likes to eat tree sap!

A flying squirrel lives in trees! It can jump over 150 feet!

23

Words to Know

den

seeds

teeth

Index